Poetry with Reason

Collection of Poetry of Life's Emotions

Thoughts and Love

D. L. Winters

ISBN: 9781073564828

Contents

The Name

The Name that men have called upon for so many years,

The Name that brings forth Comfort and dries all of our tears,

A Title that has been given to a chosen Son,

Famous by all mankind, being recognized as the Holy One,

Given more Names to express His nature,

Which He has demonstrated for us to testify,

Having held the Title of being called the Truth,

And not once has He been caught in a lie,

His Name shows forth notoriety,

And it also exemplifies power,

Being the chosen Seed of Deity,

The Spiritual Living Water,

A heavy downpour of many showers,

A Ransom Payer for the sins of man,

Has been a conjunction name like the Redeemer,

The High and Lofty One, and the Great I AM,

Him being the only hope, for all the believers,

1

The Way maker, The Lamp Bearer,

The Light and Morning Star,

The Way the Truth and the Life,

And His presence is never far,

The Good Master, the Financial Supplier,

The Healer of the sick,

The Blind Guide, to a blinded eye,

Who parted a sea with just a stick,

The Prince of Peace, the Unblemished Lamb,

Who died on Calvary,

The Corner Stone, and Him all alone,

Stands in the place, for you and me,

The Lord of Hosts, the King of kings,

The Armor that men need to wear,

The infallible Word, and the Righteous One,

Omnipresent and everywhere,

Believers will be hated for His Namesake,

That has been endlessly rejected,

That at the Name of Jesus Christ, every knee shall bow,

Before setting one foot into heaven.

<u>Following the Path</u>

Babies didn't come with instructions for us to clearly see,

The path to a brighter future and living out their dream,

It would be wonderful for things to go as planned,

That's why we must consider the challenges at hand,

Basic Instructions Before Leaving Earth,

Is an acronym for the Bible, that we may use,

It gives us some guidance on how to live our lives,

Which some of us, have chosen not to do.

We could save ourselves, a lot of headaches,

If we would read the instructions, on the back of the product,

But most of the time, we figure we know already,

Which for the most part, results in a foul up,

Google has made it easy to help us find our way,

When looking for directions to get to our place,

Often technology is relied upon each day,

Walking down the street with a device in our face,

Love is a word, that expresses feelings, which come from
deep within,
However, love did not, come with instructions, to show
us how to begin,
In a relationship, filled with passion and joy, to keep us
as one,
For the couples that have figured love out, are truly
considered the blessed ones.

Instructions are given to impart knowledge from one
person to the next,
To teach and receive a command that is not always easily
met,
As information, is being conducted, to illustrate what to
grasp,
So it's best to have it, and not need it, rather than to need
it and not have.

Inner Voice

Have you ever wondered where your conscience comes
from?
That inner voice in your mind that gives us that
forewarning alarm,
To follow our first mind or ignore it like some often do,
Making right or wrong choices that are mentally up to you,
Take for instance the animated version of this picture,
When the Angel and the Devil sit on each side of one's
shoulder & whispers,
The Angel gives us guidance on doing what's right,
But the devil keeps on enticing us to put up a fight,
Now the weak minded, are the ones that always give in,
Thinking that this little devil is a newfound friend,
But "only the strong will survive" is a quote very well
spoken,
As our wise conscience follows through, truth be spoken,
Most of us have had that guilty conscience truly affect us,
And seeing that we can't read each other's minds,
We often must rely on trust,

It is written what's done in the dark shall come to the light,

Seeing that our conscience won't let us sleep,

As we toss and turns all night,

Nervousness kicks in along with that adrenaline rush,

Constantly looking over our shoulder, with butterflies in

our gut,

As beads of sweat, start appearing across our forehead,

With a visual rewinding picture, of what we already did,

Trying to keep our composure, seems to be our focus,

But if the truth comes out, then our secret is well open,

Now there is a load on our hands, that we didn't want to

handle,

We tried to run from a situation,

That could have easily been dismantled,

As life goes on and we learn from the things we do,

We learn that our conscience can truly testify against us

too,

Some seem to enjoy making mistakes, and make it a

common habit,

But if we were wise in our own eyes,

When our conscience speaks, to reach out and grasp it.

Integrity

Integrity… integrity is a thing that we should have,

A code of values that are never incorrect or bad,

Take for instance, the lost and found department,

When we notice that one of our valuables have departed,

We may feel broken hearted, upset, dazed and confused,

Back tracking all the places we went,

Jogging our memory, on what next steps to take and do,

While integrity has worked its ability, in a person that has

presented a solution,

To settle our rambling mind, from a constant race of

confusion,

In the lost in found, where we found what we lost,

A worthwhile principle, or quality that doesn't have a

cost,

Though we are poor men and we walk in our integrity

We're considered better than a perverse rich man, like a

common celebrity,

Integrity is a value, that is shown even when people are

not around,

It's a completeness of loyalty,

That allows us to recycle, versus throwing our trash on
the ground,

This is something that should be instilled in children,

That are being raised across the land,

It's just like when we see someone drop their wallet,

So, we grab it, and make sure that we returned it to that
man,

Or maybe when a woman leaves her purse in a grocery
basket,

Which always seems to be a very bad habit,

However, integrity makes us bring it to her attention,

Of her important valuables, that could have been missing,

Now we live in a generation,

Where the faithfulness of integrity has grown cold,

At one point and time we could leave our homes with the
door open,

But if we try it now, I commend you because you are
truly bold,

It is never too late to allow integrity in our character,

A good feeling it generates, no matter what kind of
weather,

To maintain a loyalty, a common goal, that we all can do,

Integrity is a unique gift, which we can wholeheartedly

follow through.

Daily Decisions

Snap out of it!

Let's stop daydreaming and get our thoughts together,

Going through changes at times,

Can keep us under the weather,

Feeling wishy-washy at times,

Not knowing if we should go with what our heart is

feeling,

Or go with our logical thinking of mind,

We can be so confused on what we should do,

We can be so lost not knowing which way to go,

 It's a constant mental battle, day in, day out,

We can feel like a question mark (?) with a large amount

of doubt,

It started with a one-way road,

And now we are stuck at the end,

Because we reached the very part of the road,

Where two new roads begin,

We have been on this journey too long to turn back now,

And we know if we take the wrong road,

Only God knows how,

This journey will end and if we will reach our peak,

Or can we be drowned with sadness, heartbroken along

with defeat,

We have made several mistakes in our lifetime,

And experience has been our best teacher,

But as we reminisce on our thoughts,

Our feelings grow deeper, and deeper,

Forgiveness pulls us the right way,

But pride seems to pull us to the other,

We want to do the right thing,

But then again, we say, "Why bother?"

I have concluded,

That our confusion keeps us delirious,

And we are stuck at square one,

Looking at two different roads, that are truly mysterious.

Starting a Family

We strive for a life unknown,

A bond of perfection,

And a character all your own,

You are a gift from the Lord,

That some never receive,

Your laughter brings joy,

With well-known memories,

As you learn and as you grow,

Under the instructions of your guardians,

You will receive wisdom and knowledge,

On this quest that will help you with,

The challenges of this world,

And all the rocky roads,

To make you stronger,

As you go through life,

With a spirit of love that will show,

As you repeat the cycle,

Of the fruits that you will be blessed with,

You are establishing a foundation,

From the same given Inheritance.

Humility

It's appreciated by some, but not all can manage,

To make a difference in our personality,

A personality that is remarkable and not mannish,

Being rude for some, is more common than respect,

Courteousness tends to always leave a pleasant effect,

Pride has been plaguing so many,

That when someone approaches,

With a humble and contrite heart,

There's a dullness of mannerism,

And is at full swing,

No form of a warming welcome, of common things,

Humble, doing things that are, out of the ordinary for the
most part,

Especially in the eyes of this world,

Rudeness is more common for the world,

Since it is a defense mechanism,

To cover up the niceness or the identity of our heart,

And how we feel at that point and time.

As bad as we might want to react in a way that we may

have reacted in time past,

We yet and still should hold our composure, since the

humble attributes that we possess,

In this different mind frame, gives us a different mindset

in reacting,

Differently than how we would normally react, the

composure we have with a humble attribute,

Is like no other, true enough it may have a display of

softness, weakness, meekness, or

Even intimidation but, it possesses a very powerful

attribute, being able to control our thoughts,

Our reactions, our decision making at that very point and

time no matter what the situation may be,

No matter how the situation may look, it allows us to

have those few extra seconds to think and respond,

In a way that could change our future, all based on a

humble attribute,

A humble way of thinking,

A humble mind frame,

A humble lifestyle,

Humbly, bowing down before a God that is seen,

But is not seen,

Seen…in life all around, but is not seen in a physical and
natural form,

Because of the glory that is so powerful,

We can humble ourselves in the presence of the
Almighty,

We are not humble when we act or responds in a way
that is rude,

That is mean, that is vulgar, that is harsh, that is in a form
that will hurt others feelings,

In a way that is showing a response to a threating
thought,

Or a threating statement, we are humble when we are
empowered by an Inner Power,

That is beyond the natural sense,

Beyond the sense of our being able to understand,

How we could be humble in such circumstances at that
present time,

The natural sense can't comprehend how we can be yet
and still humble in a crucial situation,

The natural can't comprehend how we can be humble in
an unruly situation,

When the situation is unfair, when the situation is being

mistreated, when the situation has been violated,

Disrespected, when the situation is out of control,

The natural can't understand, can't comprehend, can't

recollect, can't decipher, can't determine,

The humble attribute that we may possess,

That makes us powerful, and stronger,

Being the stronger minded individual, wisdom

knowledge and understanding is power,

With a humble heart, we may accomplish many things,

We may be able to be fully respected in certain

circumstances,

However, we will get recognized by the one that created

the word, the meaning, the attribute of humble.

Discernment

It's a gift like no other,

A skill that is exercised by most mothers,

Foreknowledge of something without reason,

Fathers use it and are considered wise and cleaver,

An instinctive powerful natural impulse,

With sheer knowledge of what issue it may be,

A continuous pattern of which is known,

Along with learning the process of familiarity,

This Understanding has a huge void to fill,

It Surpasses the heart, the mind, a true vibe that you can feel,

Instinctively understanding it before it comes,

A blessing from the Father, passed down to the Son,

A sudden rush, to learn of its presence at your best,

Mind boggling, supposing, dealing with a mental test,

Logical thinking reaching a conclusion, honest and true,

comprehensive discernment, in a gift where we grew,

As our eyes become open and our thoughts are made clear,
Discernment is a wonderful gift given to some,
While others who are unaware, will unfortunately fear,
The result of the battle that is already won.

In the New Season

Things to look forward to… In the New Season,

When you have been hoping and praying,

… In the New Season,

For that financial blessing to flourish,

… In the New Season,

We receive a breakthrough accepting things to look
forward to,

… In the New Season,

Striving each day, doing our best to make ends meet,

Feeling empty inside knowing that life isn't complete,

… In the New Season,

Once we have stopped looking, love has come and swept
us off our feet,

… In the New Season,

The over joyous feeling of conceiving, things to look
forward to,

… In the New Season,

As that day approaches, we may be weary and unfocused,

But keep in mind, that we are of value, to not feel
hopeless,

… In the New Season,

Some struggles are to better us, to be strong to cope with,

… In the New Season,

As we learn to appreciate the things to look forward to,

… In the New Season,

Keep our hope alive and expect what's rightly desired,

Knowing that this is just a period that soon will be
expired,

… In the New Season,

From the economy, to our house, health or even a career,

… In the New Season,

Has its time to change for the better for us to look
forward to,

… In the New Season,

Freedom at last, a harvest time has overflowed this
season,

That cure of cancer, that help that was needed, that gave
us a reason,

… In the New Season,

Or maybe that job, or that car, that inspired hope for us to
believe in,

… In the New Season,

That will embrace us; grow patience in us, to look
forward to,

 … In the New Season,

Going to that happy place, just to enjoy a peace of mind,

Being able to relax and take a deep breath, to lay back an
unwind,

… In the New Season,

Wisdom, knowledge and understanding are tools to see
us through,

… In the New Season,

To achieve our hopes and dreams, as things to look
forward to,

… In the New Season,

In the Beginning

In the beginning it starts with a seed,

From emotions and pleasure,

Through vigorous activity,

After nine months have passed,

The water breaks, and relieves the pressure from the

lump,

Out you come, and the doctor bends you over, to pat you

on the rump,

Now this is your first day in the world,

With a fresh start, a new thing to explore,

A lot of crying and joy coming from your mother and

more,

As days turns to weeks and weeks turn to years,

You notice a pattern,

That seems to happen each year,

From cakes to balloons,

Toys, ice cream, and food to consume,

Along with assorted colors and banners decorating the

room,

As you gracefully age,

Some dread to see this most familiar day,

And the excitement of getting older tends to fade away,

But with age comes wisdom, knowledge an

understanding,

And you see your purpose in life,

What God has truly granted,

Happy Birthday to you!

Is a chant we all like to hear,

So, enjoy your precious birthday every year.

Motherhood

Mothers are a well spring of life,
Placed in our lives to be parents and overseers of their
young,
Some mothers carry the title of being a wife,
Joined to a man to be counted as one,

Mothers have a unique and divine purpose,
Fully equipped to protect and guard those of her own,
Displaying unconditional love that reaches the surface,
Of the hearts of her offspring that are truly well known,

Mothers, though at times may display tough love,
Being responsible individuals since the beginning of
time,
Looking for help and signs from the Lord up above,
And questioning themselves when they feel bitter at
times,

Mothers, will give all they have even the shirt off their
shoulders,
Will even take extreme measures just to get ends meet,
As children, we don't recognize until we get older,
All the teaching and preaching that kept her on her feet,

Mothers, are the only beings that have felt a life live
within them,
Taking on birth pains, and nourishing a life, to be healthy
and live,
Admiring and enjoying a life, that so dearly resembles
them,
Until one day this life matures, no longer needing mother
to live,

So, mothers on this day and everyday beyond,
We show our love for you that is so dearly fond,
We appreciate your love that you have unconditionally
given us,
To know in your hearts that: In Mother's We Trust.

For as woman came from man, even so man also comes through woman; but all things are from God.

Fatherhood

One of the greatest occupations,

That has ever been known to man,

Is being a true male parent,

Accepting his responsibilities, by doing whatever he can,

For the unworthy ones, it is oh so easy,

To turn your back on your mate and a child you have
made,

But for us that are truly in it for the long haul,

Will learn how much of a daily challenge it is, for us to
willingly face,

As we accept the role of being a father,

There are characteristics that come with the title as well,

A mighty protector in the eyes of our children,

That watches over them and cares for them very well,

Now the day will come for a father,

To pass down wisdom to some ears that are eager to hear,

As he stores up memories, as his children learn and grow,

That he will fondly cherish, within his heart to keep them near,

Yet fathers can have a different approach, to express how they feel,

By using tough love, serious discipline, and telling it like it is,

Leading by example, and showing one the difference between right and wrong,

Guiding our children, in the way they should go,

Building their courage to be strong,

Actively being a role model as well as affectionate loving and caring,

Defending them from anything that might come their way,

Always willing to show attention to our children,

As we build the foundation to their future, so that they may live a brighter day,

After all the hard groundwork has been laid,

We owe gratitude and thanks to these men I must say,

As we show our love and appreciation,

To celebrate this wonderful Father's Day!

Daily Devotion

Commitment can be a touchy subject for people without
a clue.
We can yell scream and cry until our face turns blue.
I'm from the show me state where
our commitment must be shown for me to confide my
trust in you.
But if you are naturally a committed type of individual
then you don't have to worry about what to do.

Do your own research… if you have the audacity.
Commitment is a jewel that some people are oh so glad
to see.
Commitment can be a task that some are just not cut out
to do.
If you consign yourself with me… then I will confide
myself in you.

Commitment is one of the strongest forms of trust known
to man.

Commitment has been expressed… from the Son of man.

Commitment is a pledge that is made from someone to someone or something.

Commitment is an oath of knowing that you are doing the right thing.

Commitment alone can resolve an issue of the slightest lack of trust.

Commitment really shows a person that you love them that much.

What commitment have we made?

Have we been committed on this day?

Has commitment walked down our way?

Have we made a commitment today?

When we say "I Do" in a marriage… did our commitment activate?

Or did we find out after the divorce… that it was entirely too late?

Do we know how to be a commitment?

Do we know what to do when we get it?

Can we make it like an hourglass,

To keep the time going just by flipping it?

Well let me give a better clue,

To make it stick just like glue,

Always be real with yourself,

Even when people are not being real with you.

Now if our word is our bond,

Then it will reflect what we do,

Which it's our commitment to what we said,

That makes our word come true.

An oath that was set that will never be broken,

Due to the commitment that is being quoted that was

highly spoken,

Actions speak louder than words is what I was always

told,

Did our commitment show through our actions... that

stood out mighty and bold?

Counterfeit commitment candidates are on the rise,

Instead of telling the truth… they would rather tell lies,

Let's do what we must do… to be exactly sure of what it is,

Let's maintain our train of thought…of our range of commitment

When we are committed, we will stand firm and tall,

Commitment is when we walk after righteousness, avoiding any sinful fall.

Don't Give up on Me

For a heart that holds feelings, that contains nothing,

Allows the mind to forever go aimlessly about,

Vain and vanity consumes the desire to do, with success,

After the damage was done, and you find yourselves left

without,

Deeper than a dungeon, lower than an abyss,

Can be anything too deep for measurement,

Visually witnessing the occurrence of being renounced,

As lines of communication cast off channels of

acknowledgement,

How long must we reach out in desperation for comfort?

Patience has its vivid way of building us from within,

But the desire of our heart has been seared for what

purpose?

To be disowned after starting a journey with no end.

Time reveals all even when much has been done in
secret,
Truth allows us to make a serious decision on how to
treat it,
A person or thing formally dear to us may have burned
that final bridge,
Likewise, to give up or walk away from them is all that's
left to give,

As the sun rises over us all, to start a new day,
We may take advantage of the unknown challenges
ahead,
It shall be a triumphal shout of glory that erupts from
down under,
To overcome from being forsaken, an experience we
truly dread.

God is Love

Love,

The most powerful force on earth,

It makes grown men cry,

It brings joy deep inside,

And no value can compare to it's worth.

Love,

Is the bond in a relationship,

Is shown when we're hurt or sick,

Has kept happy homes together,

And has completed a friendship.

Love,

Though mistaken at times,

For a strong care or a like,

Misused by mankind,

Who have no understanding of what it's like,

Love,

Has more meanings than one,

Oh, so bright and oh so real,

Like the heat from the summer sun,

Sharing it with that special someone.

Love,

Is what I have for You,

When I'm feeling down and out,

You make your presence known,

You uplift me with a memory,

Or a peculiar song.

Love.

Keeping Our Promises

It's already hard to deal with a promise that was broken,

Whether it was written down,

Or a few soft words, that were kindly spoken,

It can put a kink in our plans,

Or one of the main pieces missing to a puzzle,

When one enlightens us on a future expectation,

To only leave us with a burst of a bubble,

Some maybe strong enough, to move on an let go,

Even though negative results evolved,

The flip side is, we get a chance to learn and grow,

If we can't perform the acts of a promise that were made,

Why not come clean so that the Truth can pave the way,

Yet falseness finds its way to temporarily ease the pain,

But in the end... the results remain the same,

There is a list of individuals that are guilty as charged,

Dads and husbands, wives and mothers,
Who unknowingly have violated a few hearts,

Boyfriends, girlfriends, not to mention sisters & brothers,
Best friends, next of kin, an even a few grandmothers,
That have engaged in a pledge to do or not to do
something,
While trying to explain, in a few words that are utterly
murmuring,

We may learn in time that the truth may hurt within,
Knowing that it takes a bigger person,
To be mature enough to overlook it hoping it never
happens again,

Broken promises are really something we should think
about,
After experiencing it firsthand, we know for a fact what it
is all about,
We get a chance to look back at ourselves, leaving no
details out,

To reframe from making the same mistake and leaving no room for doubt.

The Truth, The Way and The Life

Annoying like a summertime fly,

Rolling off the tongue,

With no reason of why,

To some it seems harmless,

To avoid telling the truth,

If the shoe was on the other foot,

Would it take a toll on you?

Most of the time it's unnecessary,

In the end the truth is revealed,

Now you must deal with the lack of trust,

From the way this other person makes us feel.

Make a deal to tell the truth,

And never tell a lie again,

It has become a habit that we have formed,

That we choose not to end.

We try to keep a straight face,

But in our mind is where the lie begins,

We play out the lie… rehearsing it line by line,

Trying to keep our story straight… from beginning to the

end.

It's sad to say,

That it happens more often than not,

When we burn that bridge,

We get challenged and put on the spot,

It could be a life-threatening issue,

And it would be beneficial to others,

To save our life from being destitute,

Helping deliver the life of a fellow brother,

There is a benefit that we can achieve,

Doing away with a white lie,

An wearing our true feelings on our sleeves.

Making Room for Joy

Uncontrollable at times,

Not expecting to allow the expressions of a feeling,

To be resembled in a form of a soft,

Yet delicate design,

Able to have a contagious effect,

An effect, that may join two together,

With a united expression that is priceless,

Various reasons can be the cause,

Some may be of a joyous effect,

In any event,

The emotion is real,

Reminiscing on the time past,

Or a present thing that has recently taken place,

Sometimes out in the open,

Or away in that secret place,

A heart fluttering feeling,

Along with a quiver of the chin,

Not understanding why,

Not caring why,

Just hoping that the hurt will end,

Never seeing that special someone again,

Reaping an unwanted harvest,

That was never meant to take place,

Love has a way of fluttering this emotion,

Seeing a bright side,

Or the gloomy side, filled with remorse,

Time may pass,

And it yet can still be there,

Convincing ourselves,

Not to show any care,

Being hard to do,

Is a true result,

For the sniffles and the thoughts,

Makes it hard to continue,

Yes, hopefully there will be a brighter day,

For the clouds have consumed this day,

A day filled with hurt, pain, and anguish,

Sunshine lurks around the corner,

And brighter days for the future,

Once the shedding has taken place,

It leaves emptiness to be filled,

It is dry,

Very visible, when it is all said and done,

Not wanting to talk about, the shedding that has been

done,

Shedding Tears, to make room for joy,

Shedding Tears… to make room… for joy.

Marriage

As the husband is the head of the union between the two,

The wife has just as much of an important role to perform

and do,

To share a promise together,

That only passing away can separate,

For love in a marriage,

Is a bond of perfection,

A close union that symbolizes oneness,

And overflows with trust,

Commitment is a major part that plays a role,

A dazzling feeling linked from the soul,

The husband that is willing to be a servant-leader,

Along with a wife that is willing to accept her duty,

Leads to a wedlock and a thrown away key,

Eternity isn't long enough for a holy matrimony,

When we have found the mate of our dreams,

Marriage is a special partnership,

Between two willing to become one,

Marriage has its challenges to face,

But love restricts separation from being an option,

Honesty is a major factor,

That allows a marriage to be strong,

Marriage is far more surpassing than beauty,

With the melody of a sweet and soothing song,

Birds chirp and the sky is blue,

When we are in a marriage with someone,

Who truly loves you for you,

The reason wasn't based on a financial gain,

Or how the artificial intimacy clouded our brain,

How about how attractive an enticing one may look,

Or a fantasy dream that evolved from a magazine or book,

It was based on two people falling in love with each other,

That was forever willing to share the same name.

Vivid Memory

You remember the last words that were said to your
loved one that went to a better place,
A vivid vision that can be photographically remembered
of what happened long ago,
A happy face that makes us smile in the morning waking
up to a kiss that we remember,
An accomplishment that we remember because now we
are living the life we waited for,
The feeling of a child moving in your womb is a feeling
to remember,
The scar on our knees that we remember getting by
playing as a child and falling to the floor,
The sound of a violent fight, happening with our parents
in the next room, that we remember,
It was a beautiful day that we remember when we locked
eyes with the love of our life,
After leaving our keys in the door one to many times
after coming home made us remember to back track,
Still friends to this day after we remember what they did
for us when we found ourselves in a jam,

Walking in on our spouse having an affair on us is

something that no one wants to remember,

Wisdom was one of the things that we remember from

that special relative that is close to us,

It was so funny that we couldn't help but remember the

entire scene from beginning to end,

No other song that we can remember that we have heard

has the same effect as our special song,

All the fights that we remember that we had with our

siblings are something worth remembering,

We remember what we want to remember and there are

things that we would love to forget,

Memories is something that has formed our human race

because we remember our ancestors,

We base a lot of our decisions on what we remember

whether it was good or bad,

How will we remember each day that is different from

the next, we all have a memory bank,

It holds memories of someone to remember that will

remember us for who we are and were.

Tares Among the Wheat

The things that make us laugh,

The things that make us cry,

The things that make us put our hands on our head and

ask why,

The things that make us drink,

The things that make us smoke,

The things that make us make up our mind and say no,

The things that make us happy,

The things that make us sad,

The things that make us wonder why it went all bad,

The things that make us lonely,

The things that make us mad,

The things that make us think about what we had,

The things that make us cheat,

The things that make us rob,

The things that make us stronger from what we saw,

The things that make us rape,
The things that make us date,
The things that make us take a chance on straddling the gate,

The things that make us evil,
The things that make us kill,
The things that make us do anything just to pay your bills,

The things that make us tired,
The things that make us inspired,
The things that make us give up all hope and lose all desire,

The things that make us lie,
The things that make us die,
The things that make us wonder why the suicide rates are so high,

The things that make us know,

The things that make us grow,

The things that make us pray for all the hungry &

homeless folk,

The things that make us love,

The things that make us hug,

The things that make us question all the ones that claim

to love...- YOU,

The things that make us overeat,

The things that make us lose sleep,

The things that makes us wish we are having a bad

dream,

But is it really you?

Or is it really me?

That's living in a blind world that really can't see.

Can we be the people that can make the change?

Can I step up to make the change?

Or do we both hold Styrofoam cups on the corner and collect change?

Disaster is everywhere, and the insurgents plan gloom,
Tomorrow isn't promised to me, and tomorrow isn't promised to you,
This is the earth we live on... so how does it affect you?

My Son

My son,

You are a part of me that stems from who I am,

My son,

You represent strength in our family tree,

My son,

You are a gift from the Lord that was given to me,

My son,

My love for you will always be unconditional,

My son,

You bring joy to my heart,

My son,

I am your father and we shall never part,

My son,

My blessings are heavily poured upon you,

My son,

Let your steps always be led by the Lord,

My son,

For your future will lead you to heavens doors,

My son,

Be wise and never turn away knowledge,

My son,

The righteous path is the path to always follow,

My son,

Be a leader that is always willing follow,

My son,

You will have a voice that will be heard unlike any other,

My son,

Always show respect and reverence your mother,

My son,

I love you… for you are my seed.

Forgiven Mistakes

At one point and time in our lives,

We come face to face with either forgiving or being

forgiven,

To overlook a situation that has urgent need of

elimination,

And fully release that individual at hand from

punishment.

Let's not ignore resentment that can settle in our heart,

A true feeling of displeasure from being injured or

offended,

For some to remove it, it would be easier to remove

water from the earth,

Yet if true and wholeheartedly forgiven, no price can

equal its worth.

Pardon one's behavior that may have offended you,

Not allowing the sun to set, before we have done all that

we can do,

By this reason knowing that one day we too must be
forgiven,
As our actions are accounted for things we care not to
mention.

Conviction has a way of clenching a hold of our heart,
Clear visions racing through our mind tearing them apart,
Lying to ourselves can only last for so long,
It would be joyous to forgive and un-harden our heart to
become strong.

Anger and indignation are two feelings that both cut
deep,
Displaying meanness and ungrateful actions of speech,
Getting rid of this bitter thought to excuse for a minor
fault,
A beginning of a deeper cut by forgiving is a brand-new
start.

Can it be safe to say that it can be very hard to forgive?
After someone has wronged us and we were totally
innocent?

Perhaps breaking into our home or car, or falsely using our credit card,
Kidnapping our wife or kids and having no remorse for the things they did.

Breaking the vows of marriage and making us look like a fool,
Or even sticking a knife in your back just to take advantage of you,
However, it unfolds in our own situation remember this one thing,
If we forgive someone's doing, we also will be forgiven by the Heavenly King.

<u>Starting Over</u>

At one point and time, when being under the weather was
at hand,
A new day was awaiting, for a weary soul to resurface
again,

It was oh so cold, quiet, and very lonely as well,
Yet the refreshment of a glimpse of light, cured the
wretched spell,

Lower than the personal dignity, that we should normally
have,
Allowed our head to rise and resurrect from a feeling oh
so bad,

Disappointed at others as well as ourselves for various
reasons,
Gave us a wakeup call to rebuild our attitude to one much
more pleasing,

Worry has done nothing except for placing us in an
unpleasant mood,

When all it took was to be reinstated an get our thoughts
in tune,

Depressed and feeling like life has no meaning to pursue
happiness,

A secret recipe was rejuvenated to replace the
contamination of sadness,

Being anxious has only caused us to have unexpected
anxiety attacks,

That re-established an enriching restoration of wise filled
facts,

Receiving bad news from a great distance away without
power to enforce,

Renews the mind to allow us to know who is reborn to be
a power of source,

Mighty structures have been built to withstand age and
forces of nature,

But even the mighty needs repairing with a renovated
founded structure,

Walking into the vestibule sitting amongst others intently
looking at the pew,
As reincarnation unfolds before our very eyes of a
spiritual revival to view,

Mentally and spiritually broken down to the lowest point
known to man,
To be built back up with a revived heart and mind,
outspoken and boldly reborn again.

<u>Choices</u>

There is an unequal scale when it comes to choices,

We preferably want the better over the worse,

The good over the bad- greatest over the lease,

Righteousness rather than evil,

Yet evil always seems to be just that more enticing,

Choices allow us to live out the big picture,

We may not see it now, but in the end, it makes its

appearance,

An appearance that maybe the right choice,

Or a very distasteful taste- at the very end,

It's been said that we can control our own destiny,

A destiny led by choices we make daily,

Daily choosing the best path to take on this journey,

The journey of life that has endless- and dead-end roads,

Roads that may be smooth- or filled with potholes,

Holes that we have fallen in or either heard about,

Heard them through word of mouth from someone else's

experience,

Yet experience is the best teacher when it comes to
choices,
Choices that we decide to make on our own,
Owning up to good or bad choices makes us mature,
Mature enough to give advice to someone else in need,
Needing that opinion to help decide on which choice to
choose,
Choosing that correct choice makes the heart glad,
Glad an over joyous to have finally succeeded,
Succeeded in a positive way that we can deal with,
With wisdom knowledge and understanding,
Understanding the Basic Instructions Before Leaving
Earth,
Earth being the starting point of a future yet to come,
Coming to our senses is an opportunity of a lifetime,
A lifetime filled with choices, decisions
 and actions,
Actions that will determine the choices in our lives.
A prosperous life- filled with ... Choices

Day Three

The Untold Story of The Bunny and The Egg

The day that the world was changed forever,

Eternal existence brought down to earth, for a redemptive

work,

Reclaiming what is rightfully His,

Every one of his kids,

Pain was agonizing for those moments,

But it was nothing compared to what was to be,

The biggest cleansing performance,

That the world would ever see,

They still remember it each year, around April,

Bringing more showers of rain,

The rain that cleanses like the blood,

Anticipating brighter days of love,

Dwelling with the Creator from above,

He made it all possible, for you and me,

After being taken down from a tree,

He came back to life on day three,

Without the help of a fluffy bunny,

Or any assorted colored boiled eggs,

No bright colored outfits or pastel mesh baskets,

Let's not mask it, He rose, with his infinite power,

And if He said its finished, there's no need to fear the

devourer.

Before you Divorce

Marriage is a very beautiful thing,

That was created by the Creator,

Demonstrating an attitude that is always willing,

Solving problems and obtaining favor,

For the Lord is the author of marriage,

He is the author of love as well,

These two have joined themselves together,

To be strong for each other and never give up and fail,

There are so many different characteristics,

To learn and live by day by day,

A generous amount of loyalty and pure honesty,

Is a start that I must admit I have to say,

Humbleness, submissiveness, forgiveness is a few,

Meekness, trustworthy and faithfulness will always do,

Communication is the key, and keep your ears open to
listen,

Understanding one another is something that shouldn't be missing,

Affection, compliments and surprises from time to time,
Give a little, take a little and always view it from both sides,
Money management skills should always be perfected,
As well as comforting each other to never feel rejected,

Sacrifice for each other with love and grace,
Be patient, as we all are growing at our own pace,
True unconditional love that has no conditions at all,
With God's help to stay together to answer your praying call.

Springing Forward

The seed that has been planted to spring up to life,
Challenged by the cares of this world,
That will never be able to suffice,

We will rise, and run the race that is set before us,
Moving willingly towards the goal that is unseen,
For He has already spoken His will over us,

Leaving those things which are behind,
Never mind those who are blind, Unkind,
Without a sense of direction, second guessing,

Bombarding God with doubtful questions,
He is the Truth the Way and the Life,
Springing Forward being led by His marvelous Light,

Accelerated increase of blessing to come forth out of this
season,
The further we go, the closer our future becomes a
reality,
We praise Him, obey Him, with a humble mentality,

Growing from the source of Living Words from the
Creator,
Ignore the hater, for it will be greater later,
His word will not come back void,

It is ever moving and changing the things around us,

As we are being led by the still waters,
He is such a considerate Father,

There will be shadows in the valley, yet fearing no evil,
For He will be our guiding light,
To bring us to a prepared everlasting life.

Ancestry Dot Com

It feels so good to say, "Home Sweet Home",

To be welcomed by embracing arms and warm smiles,

The smell of a home cooked meal saturating the air,

As children run bump and thump followed by laughter

acting wild,

Mothers with warmth and embrace, with a stern look on

their face,

Uncles with story's and jokes, that last for days,

Aunts cooking and sweating over the stove,

While brothers and nephews are in the living room

watching the game unfold,

Sisters and nieces in deep discussions in the bedroom

decorating their hair,

Dad's in the backyard barbequing that aroma in the air,

Friends you have known for years that you consider

family,

And when feces hit the fan, the first people you call is

family,

From fights in the front yard between two family

members,

Or having to bury one of your loved ones, in early
December,
Some family member's feel you owe them, so they never
pay you back what they owe,
Family tends to be the first ones to give a person a
nickname that no one ever knows,
Resemblance also stands out amongst most members of a
family,
Playing card games, or board games, that everyone seems
to remember,
Reminiscing about the "Good Old Days",
And all the fun we use to have.

If something ended up broken, we know one of the kids
did it,
But let something come up stolen… it was going to be
some smoke in the city,
Some family live close by and some live far away,
Thanksgiving and Christmas are holidays spent with
family to be close on those days,
Most families stick closer together than others,

And if you were the only child, it can't compare to having sisters & brothers,

Wearing hand me downs to school for a kid, always seemed to be a bother,

That's what families have done to make ends meet, and do their best to stay above water,

From sharing the bed with others or laying on the floor with sheets & covers.

Trying to catch up and get a little bit of rest, as another day has gone by,

But as for myself, after all these years growing up with my family and peers,

I wouldn't change it from being a true family guy.

The Big Day

It was tough,

It was too long,

They say it wasn't over,

Until the lady sang her song,

The melody is over,

And we heard her song,

Here comes the confetti,

For the work that you have done,

The assorted balloons,

The elegant floor length dress,

A tailor-made three-piece suit,

A day that you are looking your best,

The long-awaited applause,

With a marching band intro,

You are presented your award,

And joy saturates you from head to toe,

You endured suffering for a while,

To overcome the headaches and the setbacks,

That ultimately formed your patience,

Concurring the obstacles that wouldn't let you relax,

After the drum roll,

You are presented a reward for your hard dedication,

I am proud of you for all that you have done,

With that being said… Congratulations!!!!!

Thank You Lord

If we could look through the eyes,

Of this unique person who we so dearly love,

Peering back at us in this world,

Overshadowing us like the blue sky above,

As the Lord gives us understanding,

Of knowing this unique person for an appointed time,

His loving grace is enough for our handling,

To encourage us that everything will be fine,

As we share memories, love and compassion for each
other,

Whether they were our own children, grandparents,

uncles, aunts or even our cousins,

Or even our moms, dads, sisters and brothers,

Girlfriends, boyfriends, best friends, wives or even
husbands,

Whatever roles they played in our lives,

Can never be replaced by another,

But knowing that they are in a much better place,

Living in Peace with our Heavenly Father,

For the Bible says that we should weep when they arrive,

And rejoice when they go,

However, most of the time we are so weak,

Knowing that this is a tough pill to swallow,

So today, let us rejoice with each other,

And in one accord, we lift our voices on high,

Saying "Thank you Lord, Thank You Lord",

With our heads looking up into the sky.

Loyalty & Betrayal

Loyalty is rare in this day and time,

But we can find Betrayal,

On the corner walking and searching to see who it may find,

Betrayal is an evil substance conceived within the heart,

On the other hand, Loyalty,

Is a form of joy touching our heart to never depart,

Loyalty gives confidence in others including ourselves,

When we know that Betrayal,

Hurts so bad, that we can make a fool out of ourselves,

Betrayal is common for those with their consciences severed,

Enjoy the presence of Loyalty,

In a relationship or friendship with faith that will surely endeavor,

Loyalty comes from a long line of legitimate loyalist,

To experience acts of Betrayal,

Can get us frustrated enough to clinch our fist,

Betrayal has been shown through people close to us we

know,

That's challenged by Loyalty,

From complete strangers giving faith, that it will grow,

Loyalty has its colors that show and is always true,

As we glance at Betrayal,

A distasteful taste in our mouth, at this individual with no

clue,

Betrayal is a pair of trousers, that fit some very well,

Unlike the unity of Loyalty,

Resembling the strength of a threefold cord with

confidence that never fails.

Highly Favored

As personal,
As it maybe,
He gave me grace,

God favors me,

He loved me,
Un-conditionally,
He shed his blood,

God favors me,

He told me,
How he wanted me to be,
He gave me a chance,

God favors me,

He blessed me,

A-bun-dant-ly,

He opened doors,

God favors me,

He caressed me,

And held on to me,

He opened his arms,

God favors me,

He touched my health,

He touched my mind,

And He did it all,

Unsparingly,

I may fall,

I even may weep,

But through it all,

God favors me,

I love him,

And I know He loves me,

He is my Savior,

God favors me.

Resting Place

We all know that one day will come,

That we shall experience eternal rest,

It is a decision that is out of our hands,

I believe that His timing is best,

In the hands of a loving Creator,

That has always given us enough time,

Enough time to live life abundantly,

Because tomorrow isn't promised for a next time,

But a loss hurts so deep,

Out of consciences in a peaceful sleep,

Many memories flooding our minds,

And all the fun times we shared,

The generosity that they showed,

And in our heart, we truly cared,

We might not see them here,

And we will be blessed if we see them there,

But if we are blessed, we shall see them in the air,

The fuse is lit, and it's just a matter of time,

Our breathes have been numbered,

By the Heavenly Divine,

Let's try our best to spread our love,

Because today may be our last time.

Unity

We made a mixture with each other that they can't separate.

It was us that made the connection to splice our thoughts and feelings together.

We are the circuit that it takes for a light to light up the room.

Light has spotted what could be a down fall from them.

They abandoned us and expected us not to survive.

We did more than survive, we combined with each other.

We meshed in a way that was like no other.

Our blend and chemistry have the formula of completion.

We are interlocked and intertwined like sleep to a dream.

A family dream that is lived out.

Having the combination of a friend to share and indulge in a united associated link.

We have that inseparable relationship that can't be broken.

We continue to merge and tie what we have tighter.

We fit the circumference of a circle that has no beginning or an end.

Our perimeter has a congregation that is filled with an
unconditional love, which has no blemishes.

They banish us but we join our joints together knitted
with ligaments that are down to earth.

We have become the counterparts that complete oneness.

We have a radius so large and we are on one accord with
a melody and harmony that is soothing to the soul.

Who can stand against the whole and entity, of a divine
structure that is founded on a solid foundation?

They will leave, but we shall stay, without being
multiple, but being one, in UNITY.

Cheerful Giver?

Greed... a sickness that plagues the mind body and soul,

An inward destroyer that can be very contagious,

Greed has the tendency to make our heart very cold,

And form an attitude that is outrageous,

Attention for some has been the very path that we have
allowed to be greedy of,

Consuming any and every one that allows it to consume
their path thereof,

A blinding illness to run loose on the prowl, harshly and
heartless I must say,

Drowning victims, as they indulge in greed, rudely
sending them on their way,

Greed also has its way, of being able to join forces with
other illnesses as well,

Such as hatred, selfishness, evil desires of the sort,

Not even noticing the change within ourselves,

Desperate enough to lie to the judge, in the law of court,

Money we all know can change some people,

Yet greed drives us on and on to the bitter end,

A none stop running race; exhausted; and knees feeble,

Has even separated the best of friends,

Ulterior motives, and hidden agendas has always been a thrill,

A thrill that drives us on for a greedy desire, a desire willing to kill,

For some it's not a game, but it is an attribute that is oh so real,

Doing their best, to get the upper hand, gaining as much out of the deal,

Greed has taken place in the most common places,

Let's not mention all the "I wouldn't dare" places,

Having their story strait with smiling faces,

All along an evil greedy desire is all that we are faced with,

Will we ever wake up to smell the coffee, and see what we have done is wrong?

Instead we have a "I don't care attitude", for someone
trying to tell us the diffcrence between right and wrong,
Quickly responding with that famous statement, "I'm
tired of hearing the same old song",
But in the end, the truth is revealed, putting things back
where they belong.

King of Kings

Quickly open your eyes and see,

How blindly I was not able to see your love for me,

Quench my dying thirst of love for you,

Before I die and forever lose you,

Quilt me with your love and embrace,

Circle all around me so all I see is your face,

Qualify me to be your prince on your throne,

While we enjoy each other in our own happy home,

Questions you may have for me,

That I am ready to answer at your beck and call,

Quote me any statement that you would like,

And see how humbly I surrender and fall,

Quietly on my hands and knees,

Humbly pleading and begging please,

Quivering and trembling with chills going down my spine,

My Lord, my Lord, would you please forgive me this time?

King… who can reign forever more and love unconditional
like you?

You are my number #1 protector in this life and the
afterlife too.

The Forbidden Fruit

What can we see, yet blinded, to see the truth?

How can we feel, lacking emotions of empathy, to be

able to feel?

Some are drawn away by the lust of their eyes that they

see,

Yet the eye doesn't allow us to see how lust has us

devoted,

Devoted to a desire or pleasure that seems right at that

point and time,

To indulge in a feeling that is pleasant for the time being,

Lust has its way of blinding us with eyes that can see, yet

not see,

Excuses are channels used to temporarily justify the lust

of us,

Lying can be the final or beginning result once lust is

fully conceived,

Intense lust produces an overmastering desire,

A desire that can deal with a sensual sexual seductive

craving,

Now considered an idol of the fleshly satisfaction,

An appetite that has no restraints to stop eating the
desirable crave,

Gasping for air when an object of pleasure crosses the
path of our sight,

Falling deeper in lust of love for money that's
temporarily usable,

Gratifying it may seem to stimulate the fleshly senses,

Can only drive the never satisfying feeling into deeper
mischief,

It becomes a numbing feeling when done for a long
period of time,

Visual intentions are also among the descriptions of the
all mighty lust,

Having that craving desire, setting the stage, and finally
acting upon it,

We try to keep it a secret and some of us are verbally
outspoken,

But what's done in the dark, is revealed to the light, the
light of truth,

Many have tried to outwit the crafty poison of the lust
illness,

An illness that can't be cured by a mere pill or
prescription alone,
We never even notice how ill we truly are,
Seeing that it has been passed down from generation to
generation,
The puppet master Lucifer is behind the craftiness of it
all,
For he too, started with the craving of being mightier
than he truly was,
Yet his result was being cast down as a falling star,
If we understood of where lust allows us to stand,
We decide to take a better approach and be cleansed as
better women and men,
We must start within ourselves to acknowledge a change
to be made,
A change for the better, to overcome the curse, that men
face each day.

Priceless Joy

As I try to pencil in the words,

To explain one of the most accepted feelings,

Knowing that it would be hard for me to ignore and deny,

It can be beautiful,

And shine ever so bright,

Not only having the ability of allowing us pure

satisfaction,

Good fortune it brings, presently known as enjoyment,

for us to truly relax in,

Appropriately gratifying the soul and spirit of a being,

With an unexplainable power that is so great,

Of knowing how and what to fill a void that is needing,

That's self-explanatory, without a debate,

Lifting our spirits, when dark clouds surround,

Overcoming battles of tribulations, that tends to pour

down,

Surfacing in emergency situations when help has not yet

been found,

Financial hardships are the least of its worries, while
happiness wears the crown,

A shoulder to cry on, or a pair of ears that are willing to
listen to the issue,

While relationship problems quickly diminish and scurry,

Some are dealing with private issues that call for the need
of a tissue,

As we accept a high degree, of obvious pleasure in a
hurry,

Openly and enthusiastically expressed, like butterflies in
spring weather,

More than a smile on our face, it's the breath that it takes
all together,

To have the ability to over fill our heart with cheer,

Positive is more effective, than negativity in a sense of
fear,

Keenly feeling so exuberant, that we literally glow,

Health problems have met their maker, and we have a
testimony that shows,

Successful has taken its rightful place, for a business on
the brink of bankrupt,

Education may be dormant for a time, yet has the ability like a volcano to erupt,

Enjoying that warm feeling like when seeing a new life born into the world,

So happy and over joyous, not caring if it is a boy or a girl,

For all the sports players and fans out there, that always love to win a game,

Have unknowingly recruited strangers as friends, when the team you're cheering for is the same,

Living standards for some, have been dark cold and gloomy nights,

Until that day, when all the bills are paid, knowing that everything is going to be alright,

For his anger is but for a moment, his favor is for life,

Weeping may endure for a night, but *JOY* comes in the morning.

What is Monogamy?

As I paint this picture of inseparable love,
A perfect description is a bonded relationship of
heavenly doves,
Who once have found their one and only mate,
Who cherish their genuine partnership as they express
how to elate,

Who can compare, to the monogamy, of a chosen unique
few species, within the animal kingdom?

Finding this one mate early on at the peak of our youth,
Has time and a chance to grow to learn and experience on
what to do,
Within a kingdom deep within the rainforest where
gorillas live free,
Yet they naturally set boundaries of only one mate not
easily broken until deceased

Who can compare, to the monogamy, of a chosen unique
few species, within the animal kingdom?

Can you imagine yourself, yearly taking a journey, to the
place where you met your mate?
Commonly sharing, the divine intimacy and oneness that
grizzly's bears make,
After it is all said and done, they temporarily go their
separate ways,
To meet again, the following year, as they remain faithful
to that very day,

Who can compare, to the monogamy, of a chosen unique
few species, within the animal kingdom?

Even within a pack of wolves, you have an alpha male
and an alpha female unity,
Who not only hunt, protect, and raise their young, while
defending their territory,
But they do it together, where these two have become
one, without acts of polygamy,

As they ensure their endeavor, while exerting their

loyalty for one another, in their own

distinctive category,

Who can compare, to the monogamy, of a chosen unique

few species, within the animal kingdom?

Deep within a dark blue world that is also named an

abyss within the sea,

Love has no variation to color or size for two great

creatures that are amazing to see,

To roam in a vast amount of space such as the ocean to

reunite with your lover,

As orca whales who carry distinctive markings and are

never mistaken for another,

Who can compare, to the monogamy, of a chosen unique

few species, within the animal kingdom?

Soaring high over the open plains dwells two love birds

that work together as a team,

Not only do they build their home high within the crevice tops of the trees,

They continue to construct it, to make it stronger, each year they meet,

Raising their young bald eagle offspring to be as healthy and strong as they can be,

Who can compare, to the monogamy, of a chosen unique few species, within the animal kingdom?

Picture this, as mankind was placed on this earth to be fruitful and multiply,

Who went above and beyond their realm of consistently staying in touch with one mate,

However, divorce, fornication, adultery, along with rape, has plagued the human mind,

An endless amount of generations, a divine chosen species, that God creatively made,

So, who can compare, to the monogamy, of a chosen unique few species, within the animal kingdom? Can you?

Powerful Women

For a woman of virtue,

You stand alone,

With the wisdom and courage,

And the comfort in your own home,

You are a provider,

And a role model,

And you do the best with what you have,

You are a protector,

And a peace maker,

And with the Lord is where you stand,

You are a teacher,

And an example,

To those who want to learn,

You exercise discipline,

Along with being a hard worker,

And as a mother you have had your turn,

So, upon your head,

A crown will sit,

Which comes with good health and many days,

No more poverty,

No more struggling,

Just overwhelming joy giving the Lord Praise.

Unknown Dad

Dear Dad,

It would have been nice to know who you were,

To see the type of person that I wanted to be,

I sit here filling sorry for myself and sad,

Self-motivating the best way I can to be all that I can be,

I wonder at times how life would have been,

With you here in my life,

To be that shoulder to cry on,

On those cold and sleepless nights,

Or what about when I brought my report card home,

Eagar to see your reaction,

Weather I got "A's", or a "D" minus,

Because I was struggling with fractions,

I would have loved to get a piggyback ride,

Just once in my life,

Instead, I have grown all up,

Still never understanding why…

I was just an innocent little kid in need of love,

Your guidance, your protection and support,

What you did was help me to be a better parent,

By raising my children based on God's word,

I chose not to fill them with empty promises,

So that their life would be different,

Parent teacher meeting and being involved is what I do,

Just being in a child's life that I wish you did do,

Like teaching them how to ride a bike or even fly a kite,

Or watching a firework show, on a school night,

When sports came around, I supported them to improve,

I volunteered as a football coach with a positive attitude,

We had fun going to the park running and playing tag,

On the swings, the slide, screaming out "catch me Dad!"

I don't know how some can pass up such a good feeling,

Being a provider to a kid that is eager to listen,

Some don't know that children are blessings from God,

And for a person to turn their back on a blessing is odd,

To the unknown dad I pray that you feel remorse,

And one day come to the light,

In my heart you are forgiven,

So that I can enjoy my sleep at night,

It may be too late, to kindle a fire, that was never lit,

But nothing beats a failure,

But a try, a try,

That won't allow you to quit.

Endure: #1

Endure; when it looks like it's all over and you 're the last man standing… endure,

Endure; when you know that you have given all that you have and you feel weak ready to give up…endure,

Endure; even if the weight of the world is heavy on your shoulders and you're back is against the wall…endure,

Endure; no matter what odds are against you and you are being defeated from both sides…endure,

Endure; to the point where your funds are so low and you don't have any means of accumulating wealth…endure,

Endure; while you are about to pull the last strand of hair out of your head from the daily stress you face…endure,

Endure; after surviving a major national disaster and all
you see is desolate surfaces all around…endure,

Endure; thinking to yourself why you still put up with
your husband and your marital problems…endure,

Endure; thoughts of temptation to break your vows with
your wife thinking the grass is greener on the other
side… endure,

Endure; after many times of correcting your children and
they still don't seem to get it…endure,

Endure; you are angry and about ready to storm into your
boss's office and give him or her a piece of your
mind…endure,

Endure; when you know that you are completely
innocent, and it's either a jury or a plea deal…endure,

Endure; while incarcerated and it looks to be the end of
your world with no way out… endure,

Endure; knowing every day is a spiritual battle and we see our spiritual strength becoming weak…endure.

TO BE CONTINUED

POETRY WITH REASON:
D. L. WINTERS

D. L. Winters writes about the center of where success comes from, the center of how to overcome problems and issues of life, packed with solutions. It's not just poetry to stimulate the mind but poetry to potentially change people's lives. The various reasons why, as humans, we look back at our history. We look at our current situations and we look towards our future. And we always wonder how we can make things better or what did we learn from our mistakes. We are innovators creating new and better things to overcome problems that we face in time passed to make our lives easier and better. So here we have a poet that writes about these things that have reason... poetry with reason. S.P.S. Statistics, Problems and Solutions. Problems are constantly being mentioned daily, but are there solutions that are balancing out these issues? D. L. Winters decided to take on a task as a young man to be a written solution to issues through poetry. He faces issues daily as a man as a husband, as a father and a businessman and ultimately as a Godly man willing to express his experiences that work. Why try to face issues by ourselves when there is help just a page turn away. Simplified poetry that not even a fool can error but it stimulates the mind to influence the youth, develop the middle aged and stir up the mind of the well-seasoned that have been there and done that. Poetry with reason books center on themes such as supporting women, true romance, self identity, family and a host of collected topics.